320 L

Pebble® Plus

Happy Birthday!

Birthday Parties and Celebrations

by Sarah L. Schuette

Consulting editor: Gail Saunders-Smith, PhD

CAPSTONE PRESS
a capstone imprint

Pebble Plus is published by Capstone Press,
151 Good Counsel Drive, P.O. Box 669, Mankato, Minnesota 56002.
www.capstonepress.com

092009
005618CGS10

 Books published by Capstone Press are manufactured with paper
containing at least 10 percent post-consumer waste.

Library of Congress Cataloging-in-Publication Data
Schuette, Sarah L., 1976–
    Birthday parties and celebrations / by Sarah L. Schuette.
    p. cm. — (Pebble plus. Happy birthday!)
    Includes bibliographical references and index.
    Summary: "Simple text and colorful photographs describe activities children can do to celebrate
their birthdays" — Provided by publisher.
    ISBN 978-1-4296-3999-6 (library binding)
    1. Birthday parties — Juvenile literature. I. Title. II. Series.
GV1472.7.B5S38 2010
793.2 — dc22   2009026270

Editorial credits
Erika L. Shores, editor; Ashlee Suker, designer; Wanda Winch, media researcher; Eric Manske, production specialist;
    Sarah Schuette, photo stylist; Marcy Morin, scheduler

Photo credits
Capstone Studio/Karon Dubke, all

The author dedicates this book to her editor, friend, and fellow December birthday baby, Erika L. Shores.

The Capstone Press Photo Studio thanks Countryside Homes, in Mankato, Minn., for their help with photo
    shoots for this book.

Note to Parents and Teachers

The Happy Birthday! set supports national social studies standards related to culture. This
book describes and illustrates birthday celebrations. The images support early readers in
understanding the text. The repetition of words and phrases helps early readers learn new
words. This book also introduces early readers to subject-specific vocabulary words, which are
defined in the Glossary section. Early readers may need assistance to read some words and to
use the Table of Contents, Glossary, Read More, Internet Sites, and Index sections of the book.

Table of Contents

Happy Birthday

Birthdays celebrate

the day you were born.

People celebrate birthdays

in different ways.

Spend your birthday

having fun with a cool treat.

Maya and her grandfather

eat ice cream.

Party Time

A birthday party means celebrating with friends. Emma and her friends eat pink cake.

Luke has his birthday party

at a restaurant.

He wears a funny hat.

Other Ways to Celebrate

You can think of new ways

to celebrate.

Julian picks out a fish

at the pet store.

Chris and his dad visit

the arcade on his birthday.

They play video games.

Hannah eats breakfast in bed.

She has waffles
with fruit on them.

You could give a gift

to someone else.

Aiden donates toys

to a child in need.

Your Birthday

Birthdays are important days.
What will you do
on your birthday?

Glossary

arcade — a place where people pay to play games, such as pinball or video games

celebrate — to do something fun to mark a special event such as a birthday

donate — to give something as a present

waffle — a type of breakfast cake that has a crisscross pattern stamped on it

Read More

Powell, Jillian. *A Birthday.* Why Is This Day Special?
North Mankato, Minn.: Smart Apple Media, 2007.

Schaefer, Ted. *When Is Your Birthday?* Science about Me.
Vero Beach, Fla.: Rourke, 2007.

Wade, Barrie. *My Birthday Party.* Reading Corner.
Mankato, Minn.: Sea-to-Sea, 2006.

Internet Sites

FactHound offers a safe, fun way to find Internet sites related to this book. All of the sites on FactHound have been researched by our staff.

Here's all you do:

Visit *www.facthound.com*

FactHound will fetch the best sites for you!

Index

Word Count: 126

Grade: 1

Early-Intervention Level: 16

24